The Musings of Crone, Crow and Owl

TaLona Wagoner

BookLeaf Publishing

Presentation by *BookLeaf Publishing*

Web: www.bookleafpub.com

E-mail: info@bookleafpub.com

ISBN: 9789357216432

First edition 2023

DEDICATION

To my Mom, Janie Greise, who always, always believed in me and that I needed to write. Her amazing gift of a typewriter because my handwriting has always been atrocious. I love you and I miss you every day. For my amazing Hubby, who never ceases to amaze me in his love, his ability to cheer me on and be my rock in our truly crazy lives. One day at a time babe, one day at a time. I will love you to the end of time and beyond. For my kids and grandbaby who keep my light burning. And to my amazing life long friends, Sandy, Emma, September, Venus and Lori, the thanks I owe you all for always being there for me can not be measured with anything of this Earth and plane of existence. HUGS!!

ACKNOWLEDGEMENT

To know from a young, young age you are different is hard, very hard. My mother's love was strong and I had to have worried her to death and maybe into an early grave truthfully. We all lose our ways from time to time. I have lost mine many times over my life. I have been blessed with people who showed me the ways to embrace my true purpose in life and to teach me so many useful things I still use to this day and every day. To know how to protect myself and the ones I love from sickness, disease, evil people and entities has been and will always be a life long drive. Spirit, Mother Earth, God and Jesus all are my saviors. My drive to live off my land, no matter how small it might be, is a heart/soul calling and there are too many to list who I owe thanks to for all the knowledge I have gained over all my years. And to my own gut/heart/spirit for always being outside the box, wanting to learn more, do more, protect more, I owe huge thanks to to my very own soul for choosing this crazy life, this time around Mother Earth.

Swinging

For my Anna

Swinging in the tree
Watching the leaves,
Blow in the breeze
As the clouds float by
In the big blue sky.

While butterflies
Flutter on by
And the kitties play
In the grass all day.

The birdies will sing
While stretching their wings
As the flowers sway
In the wind's wild wave.

The world sings so sweet
As we swing our feet
Swinging in the tree
Watching the leaves
Blowing in the breeze.

Hidden in the Moonlight

Feel the pull of the light so bright,
All while the dark frames it just right.

A light in the dark to lead the way,
To be the beacon until the day.

Shadows dance in the full moonlight.
All things glow when bathed in its light.

You feel your will slipping away,
To go dance with the Fey.

Shadow creatures of the night,
Make for a fantastical sight.

Follow not or be led astray,
For your doom comes from their play.

Heed my warning about this fright,
Do you well to avoid this plight.

Be sure to follow the moon's ray
Until the sun can break their sway.

Strife

What to do? What to do?
When it all folds in on you.

Do you Run?
Do you Hide?
Do you Rage?
Do you Cry?

The whirlpool of Discord
Swirling round, racking up the score.

Do you See?
Do you Hear?
Do you Speak?
Do you Try?

Round after round of Strife,
Sharpens the Knife.

Do you Fight?
Do you Write?
Do you Listen?
Do you Ask?

For the best way to vanquish Strife,
You need to LOVE your Life.

Thunderbird

A purple, gray and crimson sky
Will lead your eyes
To witness what flies.

Clouds so high and towering
A glimpse of a being glowering
Will have your spirit cowering.

To see the being that makes the storms
Is a sight that truly disrupts the norm,
Changing you inside out of your form.

Your mind is blown and warped.
Thoughts building fast as lightning fork,
Knowing in your heart you are but a dwarf.

The being watches you, as you watch him.
His countenance becoming truly grim
As lightning arcs in a sky so dim.

It all seems so outrageous and absurd!
Then out of nowhere his voice is heard
Clear as a bell and reserved..

I am Thunderbird.

Elders

My heart beats with glee
When an Elder I do see.

Often times Elders are tall and stately.
Other times they are short and weighty.
Almost always they are gnarled and scaly.
However, all Elders are saintly.

An Elder has stood the test of time,
When so many others have fallen supine.

Oh the events they have seen pass by
As countless smaller beings live and die.
Never being able to touch the sky
All while living under the Elder's eye.

I know I will be just another peon
Living out my days during the Elder's Eon.

Go see, feel, hear and speak to an Elder tree,
So to experience the feeling of being a flea.
This will help you understand to a degree
Why my body, heart and soul are filled with glee.

I am so blessed to have met many Elders.
So as long as I live, I will be their helper.

Pain- Is it Real?

Pain - Is it corporeal?
Pain whispers to the Body - "You can't handle me."
Pain whispers to the Mind - "You can't handle me."
Pain whispers to the Spirit - "You can't handle me."
Pain IS all of this.
Pain reminds us we ARE ALIVE.

Pain - Is it Ethereal?
Pain whispers to the Doctor - "They can't handle this pain alone."
Pain whispers to the Therapist - "They can't handle this pain alone."
Pain whispers to the Preacher - "They can't handle this pain alone."
Pain IS all of this this.
Pain reminds us that we can SEEK HELP.

Pain - Is it Ancestral?
Pain whispers to the Mind - "What did you do to cause this pain?"
Pain whispers to the Heart - "What did you do to cause this pain?"
Pain whispers to the Spirit - " What did you do to cause this pain?"
Pain IS all of this.
Pain reminds us that we are NOT ALONE.

Corporeal Pain can topple the strongest man or tallest tree.
Ethereal Pain can bring anyone to the edge of the abyss.
Ancestral Pain can send you to your doom to soon.

Pain is REAL and yet UNREAL.
Pain is what allows us TO FEEL.
Pain is not meant to BREAK us.
Pain is here to remind us of who we are RIGHT NOW.
Pain is destined to remind us of who we CAN BECOME.
Pain can be CONQUERED!
Ultimately, it is up to you WHEN!

Do I Scream?

To scream or not to scream,
That is the question today.

Do I let it all out in that primal scream?
That scream that will frighten the neighbors.
To let it all go and out,
To clear my head, heart and soul.

Frustration, pain, sadness, anger, disappointment...
All these and so many more,
Innumerable and unnameable.
All of these building up inside me.

Building and stacking, higher and higher,
Wobbling, leaning and yet stacking still.
From the bottom of my heart, soul and mind,
Filling me up to the brim and even
spilling over into the ether of the divine.

Feeling like I am drowning in it all,
Emotions, thoughts, things needing to be done.
All of it bubbling up all the time,
Not unlike a deep hot spring.
Smaller bubbles popping up releasing a bit of the pressure
But the hot water never ceases finding its way to the surface.

To laugh manically and maniacally upon reading
one of Shakespeare's most famous stanzas:
Bubble, bubble, toil and trouble.
Cauldron boil and cauldron bubble.
Knowing now it has such a diabolical second meaning.

The desire to let it all out, consequences be damned,
Can be truly overwhelming on the best of days.
But stopping yourself because you know in your heart and soul
That if you do, you will never be the same again, in any way.

This dance, back and forth, to and fro
The question once again
Do I scream?

The Calling

Do you follow the calling of your soul?
Do you drop all semblance of control?
Do you have what it takes to pay the toll?

These questions and so many more
Are what come forth from your core.
All due to the fact you chose to explore.

It can be, as others say, quite unnerving
To feel a deep, in your soul yearning
To find your true purpose occurring.

A frightening process at first to be sure,
Taking you down paths long obscured.
Although these paths allow your soul to mature.

When you follow the paths of the long forgotten,
It must be done with certain degrees of caution,
So as to keep you from becoming downtrodden.

Though when you DO follow your soul calling,
The way your heart, mind and soul start waltzing
Will be utterly and totally enthralling.

Wisdom of Choice

It is the way of life to flow,
To go fast or to go slow.
Flying up high or swimming down low.
Running as fast as you can go,
Or walking hither, to and fro.

Whether you aspire to be another Van Gogh
Or are darkly inspired by the art of Poe,
You mind and spirit deep in the throes
Screaming for an outlet that is apropos.

To be drawn as a moth to a flame all aglow,
Flittering about as over glistening snow,
Your spirit now on course to sow
The seeds of life at your own chateau.

Though to be drawn down below,
Into the deepest and darkest of undertows
Your spirit pulled onward by woe
This still allows your essence to grow.

Keep your mind always on the changing tableau,
For something as mundane as kneading dough,
Or meditating at a visionary site on a plateau,
From both, Wisdom can most surely be bestowed.

Sunset

Sunsets are the end. They are death and there is no way around it. Whether it be a sunset of the day, sunset of a year or sunset of a life, a sunset signifies a death of some sort. Sunsets are beautiful though, truly stunning and glorious to behold no matter which sunset you are witnessing at any point in time. Beauty is what you should hold onto so that melancholy will not drag you under during sunsets.

A sunset of the day with its beauty coming from watching the sun dip below the horizon of the world. This is what most people associate with the word sunset. A day's sunset evolves from the pure white light of daylight, into the visions of a deeply colorful sky on the verge of darkness. This view is ever breathtaking and deeply sought after by so many willing to witness a death, the death of a day. The vibrant reds, oranges and yellows all slowly fading into the deep purple of twilight that inevitably succumbs to the dark indigo of night. For the very few that get to witness that flash of green as the sun slips past the ocean edge, count yourself among the truly blessed. You just witnessed a truly memorable death for that day's sunset and it is truly a once in a lifetime event and should be truly cherished.

Oceans, mountains, open plains and the deserts of the world all bear witness to the spectacle of sights associated with sunset. All that is within your view during a glorious sunset of the day, allows you to gloss over what the sunset really is, a death of that day. A day never to be lived again. A day truly dead and moved into only memory. Oh it can be photographed for time immemorial but it cannot be lived again in real time. Photographs are ultimately only physical memories, so photograph the glorious sunset. Stand and watch the amazing sun die a slow death for that day in its robes of outstanding and breathtaking color. As the colors fade out of sight and the dark of night closes in, etch the day and sunset into your mind. Be graciously grateful for having lived another beautiful day and witnessed another beautiful sunset of a day.

Sunsets of the year are another type of sunset, another little death. A sunset of the year has become celebrated to let go of the bad of the year passing away, to just let it go. The purpose of these celebrations is to already ring in new chances for this new year coming in. It seems only a few celebrate the year that is dying to allow the newcomer in. So many in so much of a rush for the next thing, the next steps, the new year, they take no time to reflect on the year that is passing into memory. The celebrators reveling in what is to come and not taking any time to reflect on what has been. It is a wonderful way to celebrate life and time anew but I would welcome a time to celebrate the year that is dying as well. All so that you can truly appreciate, learn and enjoy all that has to die with that year's sunset.

Last of all but hardly least is the sunset of life. It seems to be the most misunderstood of sunsets and considered by a huge portion of the world to be nothing but a portal to eternal darkness. I tend to have a mixed opinion of the sunset of life. Sunsets of life are not just the physical death of a loved one but also the sunsets or deaths of journeys in our lives or those we love. Sunsets of life are as varied and unique as the beings who lived. Sunsets of the end of childhood, the ending of single life when becoming married, the ending of child rearing as those children have their own sunsets and become adults. The final sunset though, the passing away of their light, the light fading into the next life is the most mourned of them all, when it should be the most celebrated.

Ultimately the sunset of a life, the final light show for that being can be long or it can be short. The time before death is still the sunset of the life, no matter how short, brief, violent, long, slow, painful or even peaceful, it is still a sunset. It is still full of of the light we should be celebrating and reflect on the true blessing of getting to watch another in their sunset time. Some sunsets are so quick, like the quick green flash before the sun winks out on the ocean. These always seem to be the hardest to watch and bear, time too short for us to process the loss of light. Other sunsets are long, years of pain and suffering, akin to a day sunset with the colors of the sun only peeking through the occasional gap in the clouds to see the its glory. Other sunsets are true works of art because of the light they bring into our lives. These take the imagination to new heights, more like the stunning long day sunsets that are breathtakingly beautiful in the range of colors and slow passage of time. These ones tend to make us question and realize that sunset is not the end. It is a time to celebrate, reflect upon, and value all the sunsets the life has had before this final spectacular one.

So enjoy all the sunsets you get to witness in your life. The ending of days, years, chapters and the finale of life itself are all to be celebrated and held dear. It is up to you to hold all the sunsets in your memories until is time for your own sunset to happen. Sunsets are just the turning of a page in the great book of life.

Sunsets are inevitable.

Solstice

Solstice is the ultimate clock, never stopping and always on time. The perfect mark between light and dark to show the way to balance and unity. Winter or summer solstice, it matters not, because both are perfectly spaced apart.

A solstice is a time to pause and reflect on all that has come before. It is also a time of year to ponder all that is still to come. That perfect tipping point between the two when it is perfectly balanced and equal on both sides, like a scale with perfect equal amounts on both sides. A time when you live out the day knowing that the next day and night will be either shorter or longer and vice versa. Solstice is also the time on those two days of the year that you truly live in the moment because it is the end of one time and the beginning of the next time. Time doesn't end or begin but the cycles start anew that are needed to keep our world in balance.

Winter solstice marks the end of darkness encroaching in, the shortest day paired with the longest night. Summer solstice the exact opposite is true, with the longest day paired with the shortest night, to mark the end of day pushing out the dark. Both are times to rejoice and see the time to come as a needed switch to allow healing and growth to happen. Both summer and winter solstice are days to take it all in and be present in the moment to appreciate it all with the greatest of wonder as well.

Visual depictions of winter or summer solstice never seem to show this balance that must happen. They always seem to show the depiction that summer is all about the light and winter is all about the dark. Summer as a time of celebration and winter as a time of fear, when both are just meant to be times of reflection to ponder what has been, what is and what will or could be. It is truly time for the stigmas associated with each be removed and they be seen for what they truly are, the balancing of our world between light and darkness.

Balance is what allows us all to continue to live our own paths on our beloved world and mother. To understand that too much light scorches our mother and us right into oblivion and just the same, too much darkness literally freezes our mother and us in to oblivion as well.

Life is meant to be lived in the gray areas of balance, all along the line between light and dark. A yin and yang symbol is the most visually appropriate and wonderful symbol to understand this representation of balance between light and dark, winter and summer. Neither can live or even exist without the other because a little part of light lives in the darkness and likewise a little part of darkness lives in the light. The lines between the halves are where we are meant to live and walk, going in and out of each side and following it all back again to stay within the circle of life.

So celebrate Solstice as you choose but do not forget to thank all the powers that be for providing you a perfect timing tool to help keep you in balance as well.

Sunrise

The old saying "A new day dawns" is a truly astounding way to greet a sunrise. It has such power to bring in positive energy to you at the start of a day. Seeing as this was written by me for 12/22/2022, I did not even see the significance of the number correlation until literally after I wrote the date down. Then it literally "dawned" on me that this was meant to be written for this day in my first book. It was meant as a reminder to me that I am on the right path and good news waits ahead for me on this sunrise.

Sunrise, the start of a new day with its bright yellow and pink rays of sunlight bursting over the horizon, pushing back the darkness of night, is a true herald of new beginnings. Being drawn to watch the sunrise spill onto the darkened earth and awaken all within the natural world is a blissful and energizing sight. The light awakens all it touches from the stupor of sleep that lets us rest in the darkness. Sunrise heralds the mind, body and soul to seek out the new, the unseen and undiscovered. I can so see why the saying " The early bird gets the worm" came about. It allows the bird, person, being to attain that infusion of the first true light energy of the day, so pure and untainted. So many lament the sunrise though. I myself used to be one of the masses who did not relish the sunrise. I was of the persuasion to sleep late and retire late, enjoying the sunsets. Now I see the difference of what that bath of early sunlight energy can charge and invigorate me, even before my crazed mind can be assaulted by the multitude of tasks and the never ending task list of a new day.

Sunrise is also more than just the sun rising again on our patch of the earth, lighting up the eastern sky ushering in a new day for us. Sunrise is also a representation of all the new beginnings in life. It is the pure embodiment of new life, new choices, new experiences. A new day dawns, allowing new chapters in life to begin, a blessing, even if in disguise at times, it is still a blessing. A chance to learn new things and ways to do things, a chance to care for loved ones and meet new loved ones. For to have the ability to change a path, a profession, a way of life and so many other new starts is the epitome of a sunrise.

So embrace all the sunrises in your life, for they will truly bring you new life.

Soulmate Stroll

For my Hubby, Rob, MY soulmate.

When did the pull start?
Was it with the start of my heart?
An inexplicable draw to find my missing part,
To quell the feeling of pain at being apart.

Nothing calmed the restlessness.
My soul and being destined for oneness.
Searching with ever increasing recklessness,
Acting with such cruel thoughtlessness.

Year after year, place after place,
Finding only frustration with each new face.
Feeling ill with bone deep disgrace
After trying to find them with each new embrace.

To see someone in their prime
For that unique, very first time,
And know so deep it is sublime
That you are at the end of the climb.

Having found the one who makes you complete
Makes it where no other can compete.
It matters not how many you meet
They will just be leaving in defeat.

So many years later from that spring,
My soulmate still makes my heart sing.
For those who doubted, calling us a fling,
I hope for you to find your zing.

For when you find that perfect soul
You finally understand the role
Of how your hearts paid the toll
So that you can now, together, stroll.

For even on your FIRST date,
You CAN find your soulmate.

The Whims of Chaos

Chaos is always among us.
Its power must be discussed.

It lives to make the world shift.
Its goal to set the world adrift.

To set our mother and us at odds.
Just to entertain some gods.

Light or dark, it matters not.
The goal of chaos, to stir the pot.

Make it boil or turn it frigid.
Chaos is anything but rigid.

Sweet as sugar, sour as lime
For Chaos, their juxtaposition is sublime.

The anarchist fits right into the scheme.
Bringing to life all of Chaos' dreams.

An entire world full of knaves
Would be the utopia Chaos craves.

The ones with no scruples ever,
So that Chaos could rule forever.

So keep your wits about you
Whenever your world feels untrue.

Because more than likely
Chaos is messing with your psyche.

Familiar Spirit

Familiar or Spirit Guide?
That is for you to decide.

Black cats and owls at night.
Dark crows and ravens in flight.

Great bears and wolves in day.
Brown deer and buffalo at play.

These are but a few of the spirits
That guide us past our limits.

The way we learn lessons for our souls
Are all just as unique as our goals.

So having that special guide
Deliver messages to help you decide
Which path to choose at the divide
Can truly help brighten your ride.

So many superstitions abound
At all that is unknown and profound.

Fear has long been a tool
To keep so many under rule.

Knowledge is power as it is told.
So let the guides and familiars be extolled.

Their only job to be messengers
For those who choose to be questioners.

Evil they are not,
Nor are they to be forgot.
They cannot be caught,
Nor can they be bought.

So when a familiar you do see
Do not forget that they are free.

When a guide comes to show the way
Make sure to say thanks and pray.

A message means you have something to solve
For you are on the path for your soul to evolve...

Owl Guardian

When I was told to write
About a being of the light
It caused me to feel great delight.

To be entrusted with the task
Of helping tear away fear's mask
Is something I never would have asked.

My respect runs too deep
So no matter how little sleep
This is a task I will keep.

On describing this wondrous being
My job, to have fear fleeing
From the minds of those reading.

As tall as a seven foot tree
With features of man and woman to a degree
But the essence of an owl is guaranteed.

The piercing gaze of Owl sees all.
Kindness and wisdom on you befall
Even though you still feel small.

Thoughts come that they are of Atlantis
The tilt of the head, an owl practice
With some mannerisms of Nativeness.

A headdress made of long dead cat bone.
A staff is held that can be thrown.
Tanned leather top and bottom are shown.

Snow white hair and feathers flow
Down brown skin with blue markings aglow.
And soft, silent white wings to the toes.

Power emanates out and through
There is no way to deny the view
That thought to me, Taboo.

The guidance given to me
Has truly allowed me to feel free
By letting go of fear to a degree.

So now I know when I see an owl
My attention is meant to be on prowl
For an incoming message must be allowed.

I hope what you take away from this
Is that you learn that all is not amiss
When Owl has a message from the abyss.

Crow Guide

When Crow Guide said to me,
" I wish to see what you write about me."
It felt like I should take a knee.
For this seemed like alot to me.

But fail Crow Guide I will not
For his guidance is anything but a plot.

Crow has taught me true loyalty
Does not have to tolerate cruelty.

That lessons can be learned with spontaneity
And a true, deep sense of gaiety.

Life is meant to make you thrive.
Not be a race to be survived.

Crow as a man is over six feet tall.
As a crow, about two feet as I recall.
His voice smooth with a hint of drawl
and when as a crow, unique be his call.

His garb dark as indigo night
With a modern twist but not uptight.

Hints of iridescent light show
Within the black clothes of feather, head to toe.

His eyes so dark and missing nothing.
Taking it all in and still he be chuckling.

His demeanor proud and aloof,
Though with humor he loves to spoof.

Crow Guide hails from the dark side of the divide
Though his job as messenger keeps him aside.
BUT if perchance you cross his pride,
Be prepared to suffer his Hyde.

For the legends are all too true,
He will, with glee, take his due.

Though his reputation for causing trouble
Is more due to those who live double.

Deep conversations with the brave
Is something that he deeply craves.

His intelligence thrives on the stimulation
That is a product of great communication.

Standing under this Elder tree
This thought arises in me,
By which do I see?
Crow or Raven, which is he?

He answers back, "It matters naught."
"For of both I am wrought."

I can truly say I was relieved
Hearing the truth to what I perceived.

It helped to dispel my unease
That I would somehow displease.

He cocked his head aside
Jumping down to my side.

Crow Guide chuckled, low and deep.
"You are far from being a sheep."
"Even farther still from being a creep."
"But time is up, you need to sleep"

Forsaken

To be Forgotten , To become Forsaken
Seems to be a fate worse than death
For those who claim to be unshaken
Even calling out with their last breath,

Please do not forget me!
Promise you will not forget me!

Fear welling up from deep within
Their voices so full of fear, they feel choked.
All while combating their own chagrin
Not knowing why fear has been invoked.

The opposite of fear is peace.
It is what allows for sweet release.

You need to realize that fear is just a tool
That allows our primal souls to escape
From the creatures that many call ghouls
For they see us as nothing more than ripe grapes.

When we refuse to accept the worlds beyond
This allows our souls to ripen with despond.

When we are full up to the brim
With so much sadness and disbelief
It makes us easy prey to all that is grim.
As easy to harvest as a knife to a leaf.

So, if you wish to not become Forsaken
I highly recommend for you to Reawaken.

Revenge Stored Ice Cold

Revenge... Is it worth it?
Do I have the needed grit?

Can I commit to the act needed?
Or do I once again play defeated?

Do I want the repercussions sure to come?
Or do I once again choose to succumb?

When wronged as many times as I have been
You learn to truly look within.

I analyze over and over my part.
My role in that and all its subparts.

Many times I find the spot that it all fell from.
Other times I come out short the sum.

But oh the darkness that can arise
From deep within my soul to my eyes.

I have learned the hard way the rule of Threefold.
Acting out of impulse and ignoring the ways of old.

When you know you have the ability to slay
It tends to make your hand stay.

The pull to be the hand of Justice
Upon all that truly wrong us.

Takes my will to the very brink
By trying so very hard to just shrink.

It they only knew how morose
I am when denied revenge grandiose.

The fear of repercussions within ancient law
Is usually the only way I unthaw.

For when you have dealt with such enchantment
It makes you very leery to break the commandment.

So I will once again swallow down the hard rage
For it to be stored ice cold until I can be assuaged.

Forgiveness, the Tricky Beast

Ah Forgiveness... It's such a tricky beast.
It is the epitome of famine or feast.
Some even feel it should only come from a priest
When your body is finally deceased!

Thankfully I wholeheartedly disagree
With such extreme options and decrees.
Many are utterly devastated when a plea
For forgiveness is turned away with glee.

I have been on both sides of this coin.
As the forgiver for one that commits purloin.
As the seeker when I was cruel with enjoin.
Not least of all, as both for those of my loin.

As a younger, less enlightened being
I had a very hard time dealing
With the injustices I was seeing.
My sense of right and wrong screaming.

This made me quick to assume
A black and white world was opportune.
As an older and more mature loon,
I now know living in the Gray is the boon.

Forgiveness is still a tricky beast though.
For not matter how much we grow
There will always be a tragedy we undergo
And it will be during these times of woe

Some Forgiveness will have to be bestowed...

My Own Eclectic Fable

Since I am an eclectic being I wanted to change this last one. The date of 12/31/2022 adds up to 13 and it is the 21st poem, so it seemed very fitting

Being as I am leaving the age of Mother
And entering the age of Crone,
I feel it high time to uncover
And come full circle back to the unknown.

For too long my own path has wavered
As I have been caring for my young.
The time has come for me to savor
All that I have within that is unsung.

To finally have the time to study
All the materials that make me giddy.
My soul I feel has been very lucky
To have this time now to be witty.

With two lifetimes behind me now
Into this final chapter I go
Truly hoping the powers will allow
For me to learn how to grow and grow.

I relish receiving the signs
That I now am on the path
Mother Earth, Father God and I designed
To bring my soul out of its soiled bath.

I know deep in my heart and soul
My way is meant for me alone.
I now love my inspirational role
For those who are afraid of the unknown.

A word of caution I do give thee
The way of knowledge is fraught
With those who vehemently disagree
With all of the knowledge I have brought.

Balance, Trust, Intuition and Faith are the keys.
NEVER forget, light and dark are both powers of good and evil.
This will help keep you free.
For to forget this important part can be lethal.

So do not wait until you are too feeble.
Go forth and create your own Fable.

www.ingramcontent.com/pod-product-compliance
Lightning Source LLC
Chambersburg PA
CBHW051746130826
49812CB00033B/1028
* 9 7 8 9 3 5 7 2 1 6 4 3 2 *